BOOK OF MORMON

Adventures

R. COLTRANE

CFI · AN IMPRINT OF CEDAR FORT, INC.
SPRINGVILLE, UTAH

For those who believe

ISBN 13: 978-1-4621-2089-5

Published by CFI, an imprint of Cedar Fort, Inc.
2373 W. 700 S., Springville, UT 84663
Distributed by Cedar Fort, Inc., www.cedarfort.com

Library of Congress Control Number: 2017945004

Cover design and typesetting by Shawnda T. Craig & Kinsey Beckett
Cover design © 2017 Cedar Fort, Inc.
Edited by Katy Watkins & Kaitlin Barwick

Printed in the United States of America

10 9 8 7 6 5 4 3 2 1

Printed on acid-free paper

Lehi the Prophet
and the
JOURNEY TO THE PROMISED LAND
(1 NEPHI 1–5)

SIX HUNDRED YEARS before Christ was born, the people in Jerusalem were so wicked that the city was going to be destroyed. Heavenly Father sent LEHI to teach them to repent so they could be saved, but they wouldn't listen. Heavenly Father told Lehi and his family to flee Jerusalem and go to the PROMISED LAND.

After they left, Heavenly Father told Lehi's sons, Nephi, Laman, Lemuel, and Sam, that they had to sneak back into Jerusalem to get the BRASS PLATES. This was a very special mission because these plates would one day become part of the SCRIPTURES.

Enos
and
HIS NEW FAITH
(ENOS 1)

ENOS was the son of the prophet Jacob. One day while Enos was hunting in the forest, he remembered all the good things his father taught him. Enos wanted to repent of his sins, so he prayed ALL DAY and ALL NIGHT. Because of his faith, Heavenly Father blessed him and forgave him. Enos was very happy and wanted everyone else to feel the same happiness that comes from repentance.

King Benjamin

and
HIS TEACHINGS

(MOSIAH 1–4)

KING BENJAMIN was a kind and gentle king. One day, he invited his people to the temple so he could teach them the gospel. So many people came to listen to him that King Benjamin had to build a HUGE TOWER so they could all hear him. He taught them to serve, to be grateful, and to keep the commandments. And most importantly, he taught them that soon the SAVIOR would be born.

Abinadi
and HIS BRAVERY
(MOSIAH 11–17)

ABINADI the prophet tried to teach the Nephites to repent and remember Heavenly Father. The wicked KING NOAH hated Abinadi and ordered his guards to kill him. But Heavenly Father protected Abinadi until he finished teaching the king.

Alma

and HIS ESCAPE

(MOSIAH 18)

ALMA was one of King Noah's priests. Unlike the wicked king, Alma heard and believed everything ABINADI had taught. Alma ran away from King Noah, and Heavenly Father called him as a prophet. People from all over the land came to hear Alma teach about Jesus Christ and be BAPTIZED.

Alma the Younger
and
THE SONS OF MOSIAH
(MOSIAH 27)

Alma's son, ALMA THE YOUNGER, rebelled against the Church, even though his father was the prophet. He and his friends, who were the SONS OF KING MOSIAH, tried to make people sin and leave the Church.

One day, an ANGEL came to Alma and the sons of Mosiah as proof that Heavenly Father was real. He told them to stop being so wicked. Alma was so shocked that he could not speak or move for TWO DAYS and TWO NIGHTS.

WHEN ALMA woke up, he and his friends believed in Heavenly Father and Jesus Christ. They decided to become missionaries.

Ammon
and
HIS STRENGTH
(ALMA 17–19)

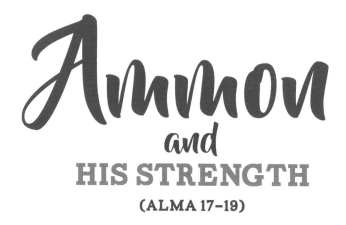

AMMON was a Nephite and one of King Mosiah's sons. He was called on a mission to the land of the LAMANITES. This was very dangerous because the Lamanites wanted to kill the Nephite people. Ammon was captured and taken before the Lamanite king, LAMONI. Ammon chose to live with the Lamanites and be the king's servant.

One day, THIEVES tried to steal the king's sheep. Ammon was the only servant brave enough to stay and protect the flock. HEAVENLY FATHER blessed Ammon with amazing strength, and Ammon cut off the thieves' arms and brought them to the king.

KING LAMONI was so impressed that he listened to Ammon's teachings about Heavenly Father and Jesus Christ and was baptized.

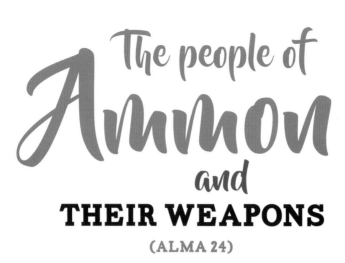

The people of
Ammon
and
THEIR WEAPONS
(ALMA 24)

After King Lamoni repented, AMMON baptized many Lamanites. These Lamanites promised Heavenly Father that they would never go to war again.

THE WICKED LAMANITES were not happy that so many of their people were being baptized. They rejected Ammon's teachings and prepared for a war against Ammon's people.

Ammon's people buried all their weapons in a DEEP HOLE so that they would never break their promise.

Helaman
and his
BRAVE YOUNG ARMY
(ALMA 53, 57)

THE WICKED LAMANITES sent a HUGE ARMY to attack the people of Ammon. They killed many of Ammon's people because they wouldn't fight back. The sons of the righteous Lamanites had not made the same promise to Heavenly Father to not use weapons. So they dug up all the weapons to protect their families.

HELAMAN was their brave leader, and he led them into battle against the evil army.

Because Helaman and the two thousand STRIPLING WARRIORS were so faithful, Heavenly Father protected them during the huge battle. Many of the young warriors were hurt, but NOT ONE of them died.

Captain Moroni

and the
TITLE OF LIBERTY
(ALMA 46)

CAPTAIN MORONI was the leader of all the Nephite armies. To protect their right to believe in Heavenly Father, Captain Moroni led his army against their enemies. The Nephites won and made their prisoners promise to throw away their weapons and never fight again.

BUT WHEN CAPTAIN MORONI and his army went home, a wicked man named Amalickiah had taken over their land and tried to destroy the Church.

CAPTAIN MORONI made a flag out of his clothes, wrote a special message on it, and called it the TITLE OF LIBERTY, which means freedom. He carried it through the city to remind everyone to defend their religion, freedom, peace, and families. The people followed Moroni and drove Amalickiah away.

Nephi & Lehi

and THE FIRE
(HELAMAN 5)

NEPHI AND LEHI were great missionaries. They taught with the power of God and converted eight thousand Lamanites to the gospel. When wicked Lamanites put them in prison, Heavenly Father surrounded Nephi and Lehi with a blazing CIRCLE OF FIRE so the Lamanites could not hurt them.

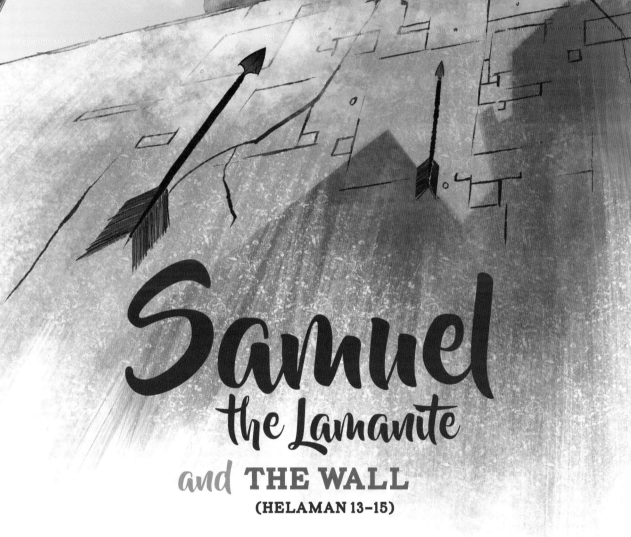

Samuel the Lamanite

and THE WALL
(HELAMAN 13–15)

SAMUEL was a LAMANITE who tried to teach the people in Zarahemla about Heavenly Father. They threw him out. Samuel climbed to the TOP OF THE CITY WALL and told them to repent of their sins. Although some people believed Samuel, others threw stones and shot arrows at him. But they could not hit Samuel because Heavenly Father protected him. Samuel prophesied that soon JESUS CHRIST would come to earth.

Jesus
and His
VISIT TO THE AMERICAS
(3 NEPHI 8–28)

ONE DAY, there was a great storm, and the whole world shook. Darkness covered the land, and there was no light for three days. The people were afraid and thought they would die. On the third day, a BRIGHT LIGHT shone in the sky and JESUS came down from heaven to teach the people in the Americas.

HE TAUGHT THEM the gospel, healed their sick, and blessed their children. Then He went back up to heaven to be with Heavenly Father.

Mormon
and
THE GOLD PLATES
(MORMON 1–8)

Almost FOUR HUNDRED YEARS after Jesus left the Americas, many people forgot Him and became wicked. A terrible war had started between the Nephites and the Lamanites. When MORMON was only sixteen years old, the Nephites chose him to lead their army because he was large and strong.

But the Nephites were too wicked, and Mormon knew that they would lose the war. HEAVENLY FATHER asked Mormon to take all of the scriptures written by all of the prophets and write them on a book of GOLD PLATES.

While Mormon was writing on the gold plates, he learned about the Jaredites.

Jared
and HIS BROTHER
(ETHER 1–3)

JARED AND HIS BROTHER lived in a land of wicked people. They were commanded by Heavenly Father to take their families to the PROMISED LAND. Heavenly Father spoke from a cloud and told them which way to go until they got to the sea.

Jared's Brother
and THE GLOWING STONES
(ETHER 1-3)

THE JAREDITES built boats big enough to fit all their people and animals. Jared's brother saw that the boats didn't let any light in. He made stones from the mountain and asked Jesus to touch them and give them light. The BROTHER OF JARED saw Jesus's finger as He lit up the stones. Because of his great faith, the Brother of Jared was then able to see the rest of Jesus's body too.

Moroni
and
THE GOLD PLATES
(MORONI 1–10)

MORMON died in battle before he could finish writing the gold plates. His son, MORONI, saw all of his people be killed in the war with the Lamanites.

Moroni was the very last believer in Jesus. He finished writing the gold plates and protected them from the wicked people of the world for many years.

BEFORE HE DIED, Moroni wrote that if anyone reads the Book of Mormon and asks Heavenly Father if it is true, then the Holy Ghost will tell them that it is true. Moroni buried the gold plates in a place no one could find without Heavenly Father's help.

Joseph Smith

and

THE GOLD PLATES

(THE TESTIMONY OF THE PROPHET JOSEPH SMITH)

HUNDREDS of years later, JOSEPH SMITH prayed and saw Heavenly Father and Jesus. They told Joseph that he would be a great prophet and that he would restore the ONLY TRUE CHURCH to the earth.

YEARS LATER, Moroni, who was now an angel, showed Joseph where he had buried the gold plates.

HEAVENLY FATHER blessed Joseph with power to translate the gold plates into a book called the BOOK OF MORMON. With the help of Heavenly Father and the Book of Mormon, Joseph Smith restored The Church of Jesus Christ of Latter-day Saints.